THE LOOK AND FIND BOOK OF
BIBLE STORIES

MARION THOMAS AND ANDREW EVERITT-STEWART

Contents

Find me!

As you read the Bible stories in this book, you will find some very busy illustrations.

While you are looking at the illustrations, see if you can find the people, animals, or things listed here.

There is something to find in every story, and if you really get stuck, you can find the answers at the end of the book.

Look at the pictures with each story and see if you can find the details shown here.

Creatures great and small

Can you find a ladybug?

Noah builds an ark

Can you see two little mice?

Joseph the dreamer

Can you count seven thin cows?

Miriam and the princess

Where is Miriam?

Escape from Egypt

Which man is Moses?

A busy, bustling Bethlehem

Where is the innkeeper?

The man up the tree

Count the four birds in the tree with Zacchaeus.

David and the giant

Can you find five smooth pebbles like this?

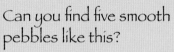

John baptizes Jesus

Find this boy watching Jesus walk into the River Jordan.

Jesus the king

Can you see this boy holding a palm branch?

A challenge for the people

Can you see King Ahab?

The hole in the roof

Where is the paralyzed man?

A cruel way to die

Find the soldier who is holding a whip.

Jonah runs away

Which one is Jonah?

Crowds surround Jesus

Where is the woman from the crowd healed by Jesus?

The very good news!

Where is the fire that Jesus made by the lake?

Daniel and the lions

Can you see Daniel praying to God?

Miracle on the mountain

Find the boy who shared his lunch with Jesus.

Changed lives

Can you see Peter telling people about Jesus?

CREATURES GREAT AND SMALL

In the beginning, before there was earth or sky and before creatures of every kind lived on the earth, everything was dark.

Then God said, "Let there be light!" and light shone in the darkness. God was so pleased that he made the land, the sea, and the sky. God filled the earth with flowering plants and trees bearing fruit. He made a hot bright sun to bring light to the day and a silvery moon to brighten the dark night sky.

God filled the seas with colorful creatures and the skies with songbirds, buzzing insects, and delicate butterflies.

God made animals—spotted, striped, and patterned; crawling, climbing, hopping, and galloping. Then God made a man and a woman, Adam and Eve, to take care of the world he had made. They were his friends, and they were happy.

Then God rested from the work of creation.

NOAH BUILDS AN ARK

God spoke to Noah one day.

"There is going to be a flood that will cover the whole earth," God said. "Build an ark and fill it with all sorts of creatures so that they will be safe."

So Noah built the ark. It was huge!

People laughed at Noah and said unkind things to him. But when it was finished, two by two, birds and animals of every kind came to him, and he took them inside the ark.

Then it began to rain. For forty days and nights it rained. There was nothing to be seen anywhere but water.

After the rain stopped and the water went down, the earth was clean and new and dry once more. The trees were green with new leaves. Everything smelled sweet. A bright rainbow filled the sky.

Noah, his family, and all the animals were ready to start again.

JOSEPH THE DREAMER

Joseph had always been a dreamer. It was partly because of his dreaming that he was in Egypt instead of at home with his father, Jacob, and all his brothers.

But while he was in prison in Egypt, Joseph helped the king's butler and baker to understand their dreams. When the king started having strange dreams, the butler made sure Joseph was asked to help.

"God is showing you the future," Joseph told the king. "There will be seven years of great harvests followed by seven years with none at all. God is helping you to survive in the bad times ahead."

So it was that Joseph the slave became a great ruler in the land of Egypt, making sure that grain was stored and that no one went hungry.

The time was coming soon when he would be able to help his family too—and they would all come to live with him in Egypt.

12

MIRIAM AND THE PRINCESS

Miriam was pleased when she saw her new baby brother. But Miriam's mother looked worried. She knew that she had to hide her little son. The bad king of Egypt had given orders that all the baby boys born to the Israelites should be drowned!

Soon the baby was too big to hide, and he cried too loudly! Miriam watched as her mother placed him in a basket by the River Nile. She waited as an Egyptian princess came to the river to bathe. She watched the princess find her little brother, and then Miriam heard her say that she wanted to keep him.

"I will call you Moses," the princess said.

"Shall I find someone to take care of him for you?" Miriam asked the princess. When the princess said yes, Miriam went to fetch her mother.

Now Moses was safe with the princess while his mother took care of him.

ESCAPE FROM EGYPT

When Moses grew up, God's people were still slaves in Egypt—and the king treated them very cruelly.

"Tell the king to let my people go!" God said to Moses. But the king would not listen. Even after nine terrible plagues of frogs and flies and biting insects, God's people were still slaves in Egypt.

Finally, God sent the angel of death. The angel passed over the homes of all God's people, but every firstborn Egyptian male died that night.

"Take your people and go!" the king shouted at Moses.

The Israelites left Egypt that night with all that they owned, but by the time they reached the Red Sea, they saw that the king was coming after them with his army and his best chariots.

Then God sent a strong wind to blow back the waters so the Israelites could cross safely to the other side. And God's people were free.

15

DAVID AND THE GIANT

David's big brothers were soldiers in King Saul's army. David was visiting them when he saw a giant of a man marching up and down and shouting very loudly. Goliath, the Philistine champion, was covered head to toe in armor and carried some fierce-looking weapons. Everyone was afraid.

"Is there a man in the king's army brave enough to fight me?" boomed Goliath.

"I will!" said David. "God is greater than a bully like this Philistine."

King Saul gave David his helmet, but it was too big. He gave him his body armor, but it was too heavy.

"God has taken care of me before," David said. "God will help me now."

Then David put a stone in his shepherd's sling and aimed it at Goliath's forehead. The giant fell down dead.

A roar went up from Saul's army! David was their hero. God had taken care of him again.

A CHALLENGE FOR THE PEOPLE

For years there had been no clouds in the sky. The riverbeds were dry and cracked. The earth was parched.

King Ahab now worshipped gods of wood and stone instead of the God who made heaven and earth. And God had sent no rain.

"It's time to choose!" Elijah the prophet shouted to all the people. "If the Lord is God, follow him. But if your false god is real, then follow him."

The prophets prepared a sacrifice and prayed that their god would bring down fire to burn it up. The prophets danced and shouted, shouted and prayed. But nothing happened.

Then Elijah drenched his altar in water. It was soaking wet.

"Lord, show everyone here that you are the true and living God," he prayed.

Fire fell from heaven, burning the sacrifice and the wet wood and drying up the water in the trench around it. And when the people saw it, they worshipped God.

19

JONAH RUNS AWAY

Jonah looked at the chaos around him. Sailors were clinging to the mast and trying to shout above the sound of the wind.

This was all his fault. He knew God wanted him to take a message to the people of Nineveh. But instead, he had boarded this ship sailing in the opposite direction.

"I worship the God who made this raging sea," he shouted. "Throw me overboard and you will be safe."

As soon as Jonah fell into the cold salty water, he asked God to save him. And God sent a huge fish to swallow him whole.

Jonah stayed in the body of the fish and prayed for three days. Then God caused the huge fish to spit Jonah out. This time Jonah made his way to Nineveh.

When Jonah told the people they needed to stop doing bad and terrible things, they listened and they stopped. And because he is good and kind, God forgave the people of Nineveh.

DANIEL AND THE LIONS

Daniel worshipped God even though he lived far from his home. He worked hard for King Darius in Babylon, and the king trusted him.

But other men were jealous. The men plotted to get Daniel into trouble.

"Oh, King, live forever!" they said to Darius. "You are so great that the people should worship you. Make a law that anyone who does not should be thrown to the lions."

Their trick worked. The law was passed.

Just as before, Daniel worshipped God and prayed three times every day. And the jealous men told the king. Darius had no choice but to make Daniel spend the night in the lions' den.

King Darius called to Daniel early the next day.

"Here I am," Daniel answered the king. "God has saved me from the lions."

King Darius knew what law he would make now.

"Daniel's God can save—even from the mouths of lions," he said. "Everyone must worship him."

A BUSY, BUSTLING BETHLEHEM

Mary and Joseph had come to Bethlehem to be counted.

Mary was expecting her first child—a son promised to her not in the usual way but by an angel sent from God!

When she should have been at home in Nazareth waiting for her baby's birth, the Roman emperor, Caesar Augustus, ordered a census—and everyone had to return to their hometown.

Joseph took Mary to Bethlehem because his family was descended from King David himself.

While they were there, Mary gave birth to her baby son and made a bed for him in a manger because there was no room in the inn. His name was Jesus.

First shepherds and then wise men from the East came to visit Mary's baby. They called him God's Savior, and they worshipped him as a king.

25

JOHN BAPTIZES JESUS

One day, after Jesus had grown up, he went down to the banks of the River Jordan. There was a man there the people called John the Baptist.

John lived in the wilderness and wore clothing made of camel's hair.

"It's time to change the way you live," John said. "Someone very special is coming soon. I am here to prepare the way for him. Stop doing bad things and be kind and generous instead."

People of all ages came to be baptized in the river as a sign that God had forgiven their sins.

When John saw Jesus, he knew that the one he was waiting for had come.

"I cannot baptize you," said John. "It should be the other way around!"

But Jesus persuaded John to baptize him. Then Jesus heard God's voice saying, "This is my beloved Son, and I am so pleased with him."

28

THE HOLE IN THE ROOF

People had already discovered that Jesus talked about God as if he knew him well, and they also found out that Jesus had the power to heal people.

Jesus was talking to a house full of people near Lake Galilee when four men came, carrying their friend on a mat. The man on the mat was paralyzed and couldn't walk—but there was no more room inside the house.

The four men carried their friend up to the roof and then began to make a hole! By the time the hole was big enough to lower the man down, everyone was looking up at them.

Jesus smiled at the man on the mat. He knew why he was there.

"Take heart, your sins are forgiven. Now stand up and pick up your mat," Jesus said.

Everyone gasped when the paralyzed man walked out of the house—except the four friends who knew that Jesus could heal him!

29

CROWDS SURROUND JESUS

Crowds were ready to meet Jesus when he came across Lake Galilee. Everyone needed Jesus!

Jairus, a leader in the synagogue, was the first to ask for his help.

"Please come quickly," he said. "My little girl is dying!"

As Jesus made his way through the crowd, he stopped suddenly.

"Who touched me?" Jesus asked, turning and looking at the people around him.

"Look at the crowd, Master!" Peter said. "It could have been any one of them."

But a woman came forward shyly. She had been suffering for twelve years, but she had touched just the hem of Jesus' cloak—and had been healed.

Suddenly, someone came from Jairus' house with the news that his twelve-year-old daughter had died.

"Trust me and don't be afraid," Jesus said.

Jesus sent everyone away except Jairus, his wife, and Peter, James, and John.

"Wake up, little girl," Jesus said, taking her hand in his. Jairus' daughter opened her eyes. "I think she's hungry," Jesus added, smiling.

31

MIRACLE ON THE MOUNTAIN

Crowds followed Jesus, eager to hear what he had to say about God and hoping he would heal them as they had seen others healed.

Jesus would never turn them away. Now they had followed him to a lonely place, and when he had finished teaching them and healing them, his friends told him that they should be sent away. It was late and they needed to eat.

"Surely you can find food for everyone here?" asked Jesus. The disciples looked at the crowd. At least five thousand people were there!

A boy came forward with his lunch of five small rolls and two little fish. He was happy to share it.

Jesus thanked the boy and thanked God for the food. Then he shared it with his friends. And everyone had enough to eat. There were even twelve baskets of leftovers collected. It was a miracle!

33

THE MAN WHO CLIMBED A TREE

Zacchaeus lived in Jericho. He was rich—very rich. He earned his money collecting taxes for the Romans—and by keeping some of the money for himself!

When Zacchaeus heard that Jesus had come to Jericho, he wanted to see him too. But he was not the only one. Crowds lined the streets.

Zacchaeus was too short to see over the heads of the people—and no one would let him through. So he climbed into the branches of a fig tree. Now he had a better view than anyone!

But Jesus could see Zacchaeus too.

"Hello, Zacchaeus!" said Jesus. "I thought I might come to your house today."

Zacchaeus was a changed man when he met Jesus.

"I want to give away half of all I have to the poor," he said. "And if anyone thinks I have cheated them—well, I will pay them four times as much!"

Jesus smiled. "This is why I am here," he said.

36

JESUS THE KING

It was almost time to celebrate the Passover feast in Jerusalem.

Jesus wanted to enter the city riding on a donkey. His friends went to collect a young colt for him. Then Jesus made the journey toward the city gates, riding on the donkey's back.

Some of the people in the streets already knew Jesus. They had seen the people he had healed. They had heard him talk about how much God loved them. They spread their cloaks on the ground in front of him. They waved palm branches.

"Hooray for Jesus the King!" they cheered.

"Here comes Jesus our King!"

But there were others, religious leaders among them, who were unhappy. They didn't like the way people listened to Jesus instead of to their own teaching. They began to plot together. They needed to find a way to make sure that Jesus didn't cause any more trouble for them.

A CRUEL WAY TO DIE

Jesus had twelve special friends, but one of them, Judas, decided to betray Jesus to the religious leaders for thirty pieces of silver. Now the leaders could arrest Jesus!

While he was praying, soldiers came for Jesus and took him to Pontius Pilate, the Roman governor, to be questioned. Pilate could not find Jesus guilty of any crime. He did not want to be guilty of the death of an innocent man.

He went to the angry crowd outside and asked them what he should do with Jesus.

"Crucify him!" came the answer. "Crucify him!"

So on a Friday morning, Pilate washed his hands of the decision to have Jesus crucified. He turned away as Jesus was beaten and made to carry a huge piece of wood along the streets to a place outside the city walls.

Then Jesus was nailed to a cross between two criminals and left to die.

THE VERY GOOD NEWS!

Jesus died on the cross and was buried in a borrowed tomb.

But then a miracle happened! Early on Sunday morning, some of his friends found the tomb empty.

Mary Magdalene met Jesus—and saw that now he was alive! And Jesus came to see the disciples by appearing suddenly in a locked room!

Jesus was alive. There was no doubt about it—he had risen from the dead! His friends saw him. Hundreds of people who had known him while he was with them every day saw him.

On some days, Jesus came and talked with them. On other days, they waited but he did not come.

Then one night seven of the disciples went fishing. They fished all night, but by sunrise they had still caught nothing. But Jesus was there on the shore in the morning. He directed them to a huge catch of fish—and then they all had a barbecue breakfast together.

CHANGED LIVES

Jesus went back to his Father in heaven—but not before promising that he would send his Holy Spirit to be with his friends.

The Holy Spirit came to them when they were in Jerusalem during the festival of Pentecost. People from all over the world were there, speaking many different languages.

The disciples heard a sound like the wind. They were touched by flames of fire. Then they knew they had the power to do anything God wanted them to do!

"Tell God you are sorry for all the bad things you've done," Peter told a huge crowd. "Trust Jesus. He welcomes anyone who wants to be God's friend."

Over three thousand people became friends of Jesus that day. They became known as Christians. They shared everything they owned and learned to look after each other, just as Jesus had taught them. And when they went home, they took the message about Jesus with them to all the people they met.

43

DID YOU FIND...?

6-7
Did you find
a ladybug?

8-9
Did you find
the mice?

10-11
Did you find
the thin cows?

12-13
Did you find
Miriam?

14-15
Did you find
Moses?

16-17
Did you find the
five smooth stones?

18-19
Did you find the king?

20-21
Did you find Jonah?

22-23
Did you find
Daniel
praying?

24-25
Did you find the innkeeper?

26-27
Did you find the boy watching Jesus?

28-29
Did you find the paralyzed man?

30-31
Did you find the woman who had been healed?

32-33
Did you find the boy with the food?

34-35
Did you find the four birds?

36-37
Did you find the boy waving the palm branch?

38-39
Did you find the soldier?

40-41
Did you find the campfire?

42-43
Did you find Peter?

Published in 2013 in the U.S. and Canada by
The Word Among Us Press
Frederick, Maryland
www.wau.org
ISBN: 978-1-59325-230-4

Copyright © 2013 Anno Domini Publishing
www.ad-publishing.com
Text copyright © 2013 Marion Thomas
Illustrations copyright © 2013 Andrew Everitt-Stewart

Editorial Director: Annette Reynolds
Art Director: Gerald Rogers
Pre-production Manager: Krystyna Hewitt
Production Manager: John Laister

Printed and bound in China
July 2014